T0390006

INDIANAPOLIS COLTS

MATT SCHEFF

Apex is distributed by North Star Editions:
sales@northstareditions.com | 888-417-0195

Produced for Apex by Red Line Editorial.

Photographs ©: Zach Bolinger/AP Images, cover, 1; AJ Mast/AP Images, 4–5, 58–59; Andy Lyons/Getty Images Sport/Getty Images, 6–7, 38–39; Vernon Biever/AP Images, 8–9; AP Images, 10–11; Herb Scharfman/ Sports Imagery/Getty Images Sport/Getty Images, 12–13; Focus On Sport/ Getty Images Sport/Getty Images, 14–15, 16–17, 19, 26–27; Bettmann/ Getty Images, 20–21; Robert Riger/Getty Images Sport/Getty Images, 22–23; Don Larson/Getty Images Sport/Getty Images, 24–25; Elsa/Getty Images Sport/Getty Images, 28–29; Matt Detrich/Getty Images Sport/ Getty Images, 30–31; Jonathan Daniel/Getty Images Sport/Getty Images, 32–33; Doug Pensinger/Getty Images Sport/Getty Images, 34–35, 42–43; Al Messerschmidt/AP Images, 37, 57; Allen Kee/NFLPhotoLibrary/Getty Images Sport/Getty Images, 40–41; Jeffrey Brown/Icon Sportswire, 44–45, 48–49; Michael Hickey/Getty Images Sport/Getty Images, 47, 50–51; Shutterstock Images, 52–53; Stacy Revere/Getty Images Sport/Getty Images, 54–55

Library of Congress Control Number: 2024940031

ISBN
979-8-89250-152-1 (hardcover)
979-8-89250-169-9 (paperback)
979-8-89250-293-1 (ebook pdf)
979-8-89250-186-6 (hosted ebook)

Printed in the United States of America
Mankato, MN
012025

NOTE TO PARENTS AND EDUCATORS

Apex books are designed to build literacy skills in striving readers. Exciting, high-interest content attracts and holds readers' attention. The text is carefully leveled to allow students to achieve success quickly.

TABLE OF CONTENTS

CHAPTER 1

COLTS NATION

A sea of fans rise to their feet. They are dressed in blue and white. The Indianapolis Colts are marching down the field. The noise in the stadium grows. Time is running out. And the Colts need a touchdown.

The Colts' stadium holds approximately 67,000 fans.

Jonathan Taylor runs for a fourth-quarter touchdown in a 2021 game against the New England Patriots.

The quarterback takes the snap. He hands the ball to running back Jonathan Taylor. The defense crashes in from all sides. But Taylor reacts quickly. He dodges one tackler. He spins around another. Suddenly, he's loose. Taylor sprints down the field. It's a touchdown! The crowd goes wild.

CHAPTER 2

EARLY HISTORY

The Colts started playing in 1953. Back then, the team was based in Baltimore, Maryland. Like many new teams, the Colts struggled at first. But before long, Baltimore became an NFL power.

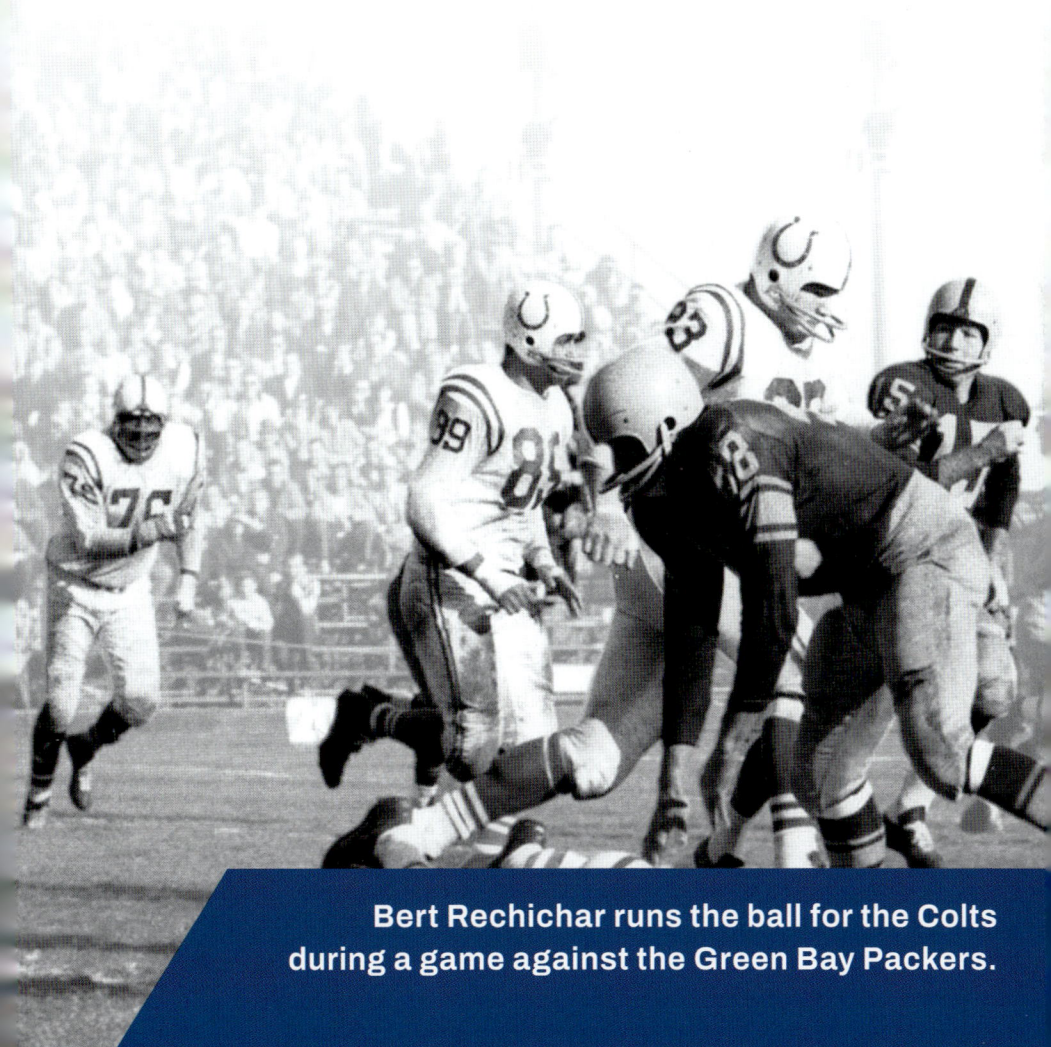

Bert Rechichar runs the ball for the Colts during a game against the Green Bay Packers.

In 1958, the Colts reached the NFL title game. Quarterback Johnny Unitas led a powerful offense. Baltimore beat the New York Giants in overtime. In 1959, the two teams faced off in a rematch. The Colts won again.

THE FIRST COLTS

An earlier team called the Baltimore Colts began playing in 1947. At first, the team played in the AAFC. This league was separate from the NFL. In 1950, Baltimore joined the NFL. But the team didn't last long. It folded after the season was over.

Alan Ameche plunges over the goal line to score the winning touchdown in the 1958 NFL title game.

Tom Matte scores a touchdown during Baltimore's win over the Cleveland Browns in the 1968 NFL title game.

In 1968, Baltimore crushed the Cleveland Browns 34–0 in the NFL title game. Two weeks later, the Colts faced the New York Jets in the Super Bowl. The Jets were champions of the AFL. This league was separate from the NFL. Most people thought the Colts would win easily. But the Jets came out on top. It was one of the biggest upsets in football history.

The Colts got another shot in the 1970 season. This time, they faced the Dallas Cowboys in the Super Bowl. It was a close game. Baltimore won 16–13. Colts tight end John Mackey led the way. He scored on a 75-yard touchdown catch.

Backup quarterback Earl Morrall (15) led the Colts to a Super Bowl victory after starter Johnny Unitas got hurt.

Running back Eric Dickerson looks for a running lane during a 1987 game against the New England Patriots.

By the early 1980s, the team's owner was unhappy with the old stadium in Baltimore. So, in 1984, he moved the team to Indianapolis. However, the results on the field didn't change much. The Colts continued to struggle through most of the 1980s and 1990s.

A SHOCKING MOVE

The Colts' move to Indianapolis shocked many fans. The team secretly loaded up moving trucks. They left Baltimore in the middle of the night on March 28, 1984. After that, Baltimore went 12 years without an NFL team. But in 1996, the city got the Ravens.

JOHNNY UNITAS

The Pittsburgh Steelers selected Johnny Unitas in the 1955 draft. But they cut him before he played a game. Unitas joined the Colts the next year. He was a backup at first. But by the end of the season, he had become the starter. In 1957, Unitas led the NFL in passing yards. He led in passing touchdowns, too. Unitas was just getting started.

In 1958, Unitas helped the Colts win the NFL title. He did it again in 1959. Unitas also won the NFL's Most Valuable Player (MVP) Award three times.

JOHNNY UNITAS THREW FOR 39,768 YARDS DURING HIS 17 YEARS WITH THE COLTS.

CHAPTER 3

LEGENDS

In the 1950s, Baltimore's defense was loaded with talent. Defensive linemen Art Donovan and Gino Marchetti led the way. Donovan used his size and strength to blast through blockers. Marchetti was a speedy pass rusher. His ability to tackle the quarterback made him a terror on defense.

Gino Marchetti (white jersey) tries to block a pass during the 1958 NFL title game.

Lenny Moore (24) made the Pro Bowl seven times during his 12-year career.

Johnny Unitas had several weapons on offense. Lenny Moore played both running back and receiver. His speed made him a threat to score on just about any play. John Mackey was one of the NFL's best pass-catching tight ends. And Raymond Berry was an excellent route-runner.

BEST EVER?

The 1958 NFL title game became known as the "Greatest Game Ever Played." It was a tight battle. Unitas led a last-minute drive to tie the game. That led to the first overtime in NFL history. The Colts scored again to win the game 23–17.

In the 1980s, Eric Dickerson was one of the NFL's best running backs. He started his career with the Los Angeles Rams. But in 1987, the Colts made a huge trade to get him. Dickerson was a fast and powerful runner. In 1988, he racked up 1,659 yards on the ground. That led the NFL.

Eric Dickerson ran for 5,194 yards in his five years with the Colts.

Dickerson left after the 1991 season. It didn't take long for the Colts to find a new star running back. The team drafted Marshall Faulk in 1994. Faulk was an excellent runner. He was also a great pass-catcher. In 1998, he led the team in both rushing and receiving.

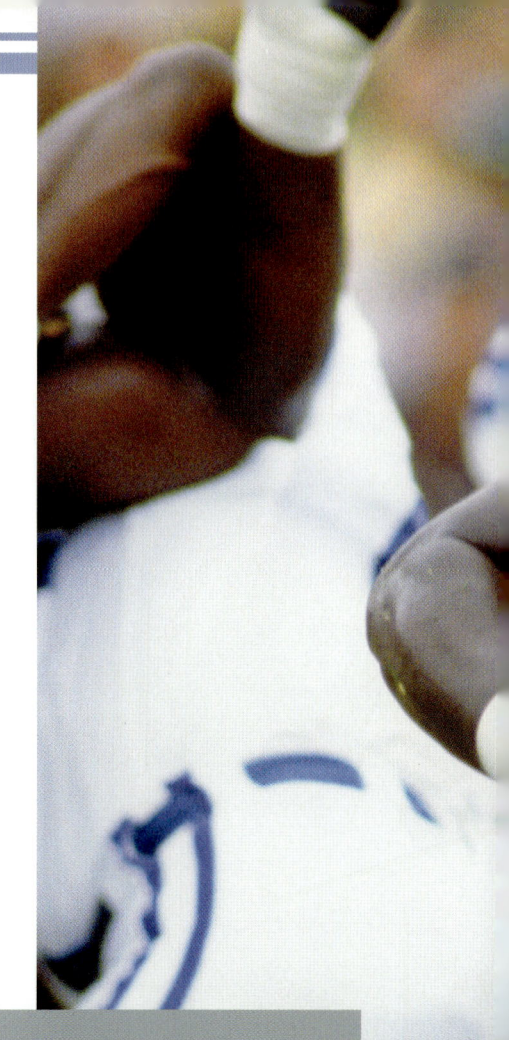

CAPTAIN COMEBACK

In the 1990s, quarterback Jim Harbaugh earned the nickname "Captain Comeback." He led the Colts to several wins after the team had been trailing. Later, Harbaugh became a successful head coach. He spent four years with the San Francisco 49ers. Then he went to the University of Michigan. In 2024, he joined the Los Angeles Chargers.

Marshall Faulk won the Offensive Rookie of the Year Award in 1994.

CHAPTER 4

RECENT HISTORY

In 1997, the Colts went 3–13. They were the NFL's worst team that year. But they got the top pick in the 1998 draft. Indianapolis chose quarterback Peyton Manning. In 2002, head coach Tony Dungy joined the team. Manning and Dungy turned the Colts into winners.

Peyton Manning was known for changing plays at the line of scrimmage.

Colts defensive back Kelvin Hayden (26) returns an interception for a touchdown in the Super Bowl.

In the 2006 season, the Colts reached the conference title game. They faced the New England Patriots. Colts running back Joseph Addai scored the winning touchdown with just one minute to go. Two weeks later, Indianapolis met the Chicago Bears in the Super Bowl. The Colts won 29–17.

FIERCE RIVALS

In the 2000s, the Colts and the Patriots had one of the NFL's best rivalries. They met in the playoffs several times. Fans loved watching Peyton Manning face off against Patriots quarterback Tom Brady.

Wide receiver Pierre Garçon (85) pulls down a touchdown catch in the 2009 conference title game.

Dungy left the Colts after the 2008 season. Jim Caldwell replaced him. In 2009, Caldwell led the Colts to another great season. The team made it back to the Super Bowl. But this time, Indianapolis fell to the New Orleans Saints.

MOVING ON

Peyton Manning missed the 2011 season with a neck injury. The team went 2–14. Once again, the Colts got the top pick in the draft. They chose quarterback Andrew Luck. The team released Manning.

In 2014, Andrew Luck led the Colts to the conference championship game. However, they lost to New England. After that, injuries slowed Luck down. In 2019, he retired to focus on his health. The Colts struggled to find a replacement. In 2023, they drafted Anthony Richardson. Fans loved his ability to run as well as pass.

Andrew Luck looks for a receiver during a playoff game against the Denver Broncos.

PEYTON MANNING

Peyton Manning came from a football family. His father, Archie, played in the NFL. So did his younger brother, Eli. Most fans agree that Peyton was the best of the three.

Manning was a pocket passer. He used his strong arm and sharp mind to attack defenses. Manning won four MVP Awards with the Colts. He also won a Super Bowl.

PEYTON MANNING THREW FOR 54,828 YARDS DURING HIS TIME WITH THE COLTS.

Manning ended his career with the Denver Broncos. He won another Super Bowl and another MVP Award.

CHAPTER 5

MODERN STARS

Peyton Manning led a powerful offense in the 2000s. His favorite targets included wide receivers Marvin Harrison and Reggie Wayne. Manning and Harrison connected for 112 touchdown passes. That's the most ever by a quarterback-receiver duo.

Marvin Harrison recorded 14,580 receiving yards during his 13-year career.

Edgerrin James scored 75 touchdowns during his seven seasons with the Colts.

Edgerrin James was the team's top running back in the 2000s. His quickness helped him dodge tackles. Once he was free, his speed made him hard to catch. Center Jeff Saturday led a strong offensive line. These blockers opened up running lanes for James. They also protected Manning.

SACK MASTER

Dwight Freeney was the heart of the Colts defense. The defensive end combined strength and speed. At times, he seemed impossible to block. Freeney spent 11 years with the Colts. In that time, he recorded 107.5 sacks.

Andrew Luck was the total package at quarterback. He was big, strong, and smart. He understood what the defense was going to do. He could also make quick throws. Luck made the Pro Bowl in four of his six seasons.

DEFENSIVE STAR

Defensive end Robert Mathis was a master at causing fumbles. In 2013, he forced 10 of them. He also had 19.5 sacks that year. Both numbers led the league.

Robert Mathis knocks down the Chicago Bears quarterback in the Super Bowl.

Anthony Richardson (5) celebrates a touchdown during a 2023 game against the Los Angeles Rams.

In the 2020s, the Colts focused on young talent. Jonathan Taylor quickly became the team's top running back. Michael Pittman emerged as the team's leading receiver.

Quarterback Anthony Richardson joined the Colts in 2023. As a rookie, he had four rushing touchdowns in his first three games. An injury ended Richardson's season early. But Colts fans hoped he would soon lead the team back to glory.

PLAYER SPOTLIGHT

JONATHAN TAYLOR

The Colts drafted running back Jonathan Taylor in 2020. Taylor was an instant star. He ran for 11 touchdowns as a rookie. He was even better in 2021. His 1,811 rushing yards led the NFL. So did his 18 rushing touchdowns.

Taylor became known for pounding defenses. He could wear out tacklers. He was also fast. When he got into open space, it became a race to the end zone. Injuries slowed Taylor in 2022 and 2023. But when he was on the field, he was one of the league's best players.

JONATHAN TAYLOR SCORED 44 TOUCHDOWNS IN HIS FIRST FOUR YEARS WITH INDIANAPOLIS.

CHAPTER 6

TEAM TRIVIA

A large anvil sits in the Colts' home stadium. Before each home game, the Colts "ring the anvil" to pump up the crowd. Former players often get the honor. They slam a huge hammer down onto the anvil.

Former Colts receiver Reggie Wayne rings the anvil before a game in 2017.

Blue carries a Colts flag onto the field to pump up the crowd before a game.

The Colts' mascot is a horse named Blue. He wears a white Colts jersey with a horseshoe on the front. Blue joined the team in 2006. That was the same season the Colts beat the Bears in the Super Bowl. In 2020, Blue became a member of the Mascot Hall of Fame.

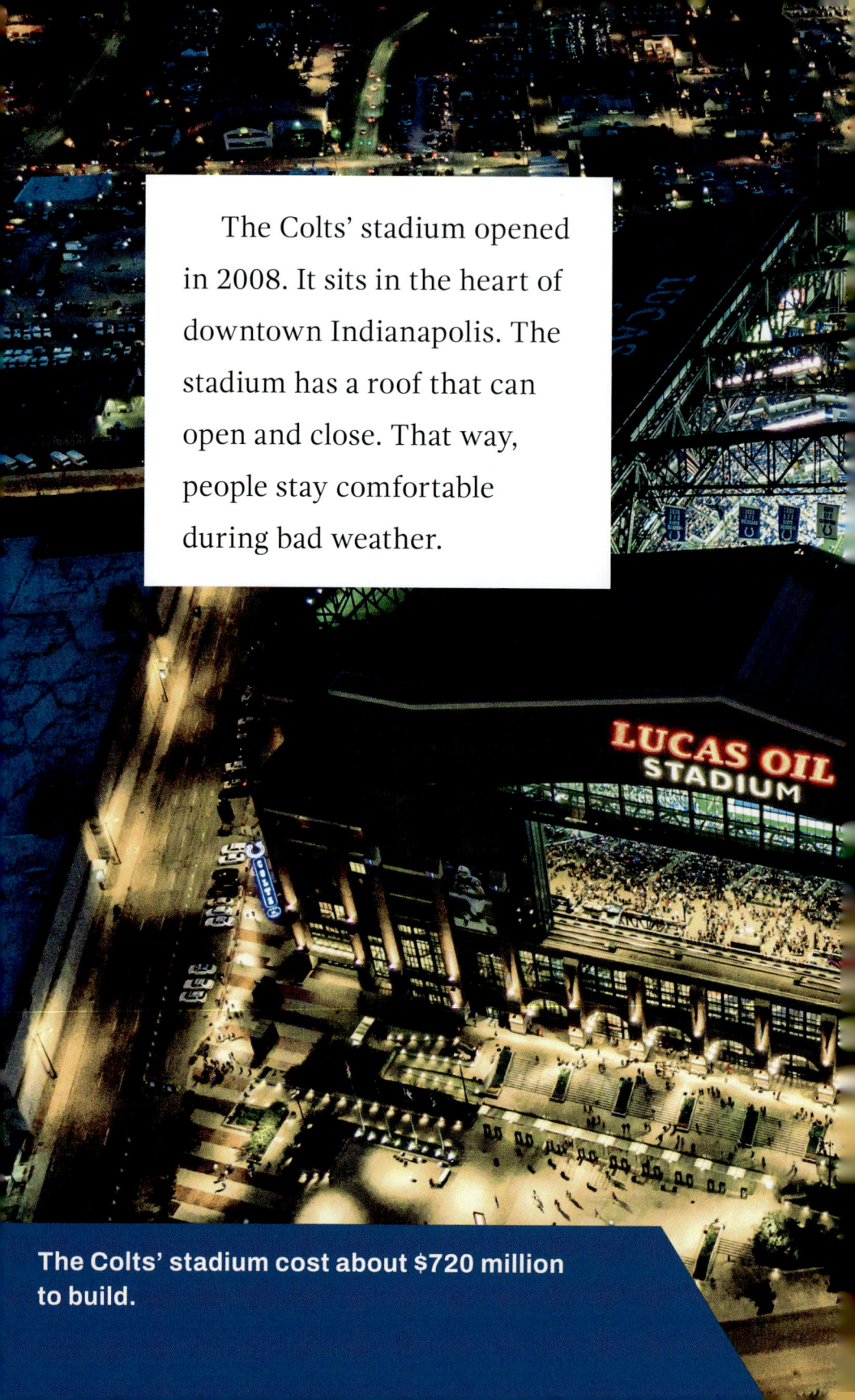

The Colts' stadium opened in 2008. It sits in the heart of downtown Indianapolis. The stadium has a roof that can open and close. That way, people stay comfortable during bad weather.

The Colts' stadium cost about $720 million to build.

BIG SCREEN

The Colts have one of the biggest video screens in the NFL. It is actually made up of three screens that sit side by side. Together, they measure 97 feet (30 m) wide. And they are 53 feet (16 m) high.

Tailgating is a tradition for Colts fans. Hours before each home game, fans gather in parking lots near the stadium. They grill burgers, hot dogs, and other food.

Some fans play games outside the stadium before the football game begins.

TEAM RECORDS

All-Time Passing Yards: 54,828
Peyton Manning (1998–2010)

All-Time Touchdown Passes: 399
Peyton Manning (1998–2010)

All-Time Rushing Yards: 9,226
Edgerrin James (1999–2005)

All-Time Receiving Yards: 14,580
Marvin Harrison (1996–2008)

All-Time Interceptions: 57
Bobby Boyd (1960–68)

All-Time Sacks: 123
Robert Mathis (2003–16)

All-Time Scoring: 1,515
Adam Vinatieri (2006–19)

All-Time Coaching Wins: 85
Tony Dungy (2002–08)

NFL Titles: 2
(1958, 1959)

Super Bowl Titles: 2
(1970, 2006)

All statistics are accurate through 2023.

TIMELINE

1953

1958

1959

1970

1984

The Baltimore Colts join the NFL.

The Colts beat the Giants again to win a second straight championship.

The Colts move to Indianapolis.

The Colts beat the New York Giants in overtime to win their first NFL title.

The Colts win their first Super Bowl, beating the Dallas Cowboys 16–13.

1998

2006

2012

2014

2023

The Colts beat the Chicago Bears 29–17 to win their second Super Bowl title.

Luck leads the Colts to the conference title game, but they lose to the New England Patriots.

The Colts draft quarterback Peyton Manning.

The Colts release Manning and draft quarterback Andrew Luck.

The Colts draft quarterback Anthony Richardson.

COMPREHENSION QUESTIONS

Write your answers on a separate piece of paper.

1. Write a paragraph that explains the main ideas of Chapter 2.

2. Who do you think was the greatest player in Colts history? Why?

3. Which quarterback led the Colts to their first NFL title?
   A. Anthony Richardson
   B. Peyton Manning
   C. Johnny Unitas

4. Why were many fans shocked when the Colts moved to Indianapolis?
   A. The team didn't give any warning about the move.
   B. The city of Baltimore didn't have enough football fans.
   C. The NFL forced the team to leave Baltimore.

5. What does **upsets** mean in this book?

*Most people thought the Colts would win easily. But the Jets came out on top. It was one of the biggest **upsets** in football history.*

    A. games that end in a tie
    B. victories that most fans expected
    C. unexpected losses

6. What does **rivalries** mean in this book?

*In the 2000s, the Colts and the Patriots had one of the NFL's best **rivalries**. They met in the playoffs several times.*

    A. ongoing competitions
    B. stadiums where teams play
    C. teams with losing records

Answer key on page 64.

GLOSSARY

anvil
A steel or iron block on which metal is hammered and shaped.

conference
A group of teams that make up part of a sports league.

draft
A system that lets teams select new players coming into the league.

retired
Ended one's career.

rookie
An athlete in his or her first year as a professional player.

route
The path that a receiver follows to get open and catch the ball.

sacks
Plays that happen when a defender tackles the quarterback before he can throw the ball.

snap
The start of each play, when the center passes the ball back to the quarterback.

tailgating
The act of gathering in a parking lot before a game, usually with food.

tradition
A way of doing something that is passed down over many years.

TO LEARN MORE

BOOKS

Coleman, Ted. *Indianapolis Colts All-Time Greats*. Mendota Heights, MN: Press Box Books, 2022.

Downs, Kieran. *The Indianapolis Colts*. Minneapolis: Bellwether Media, 2024.

Leed, Percy. *Peyton Manning: Most Valuable Quarterback*. Minneapolis: Lerner Publications, 2022.

ONLINE RESOURCES

Visit **www.apexeditions.com** to find links and resources related to this title.

ABOUT THE AUTHOR

Matt Scheff is an author and artist living in Alaska. He enjoys mountain climbing, fishing, and curling up with his two Siberian huskies to watch sports.

INDEX

ANSWER KEY:
1. Answers will vary; 2. Answers will vary; 3. C; 4. A; 5. C; 6. A